ELTON JOHN GREATEST HITS 1970-2002

PIANO • VOCAL • GUITAR

W9-DHN-446

ISBN 978-0-634-08373-0

HAL•LEONARD®
CORPORATION
7777 W. BLUEMOUND RD. P.O. BOX 13819 MILWAUKEE, WI 53213

For all works contained herein:
Unauthorized copying, arranging, adapting, recording or public performance is an infringement of copyright.
Infringers are liable under the law.

Visit Hal Leonard Online at
www.halleonard.com

CONTENTS

YOUR SONG

Words and Music by ELTON JOHN
and BERNIE TAUPIN

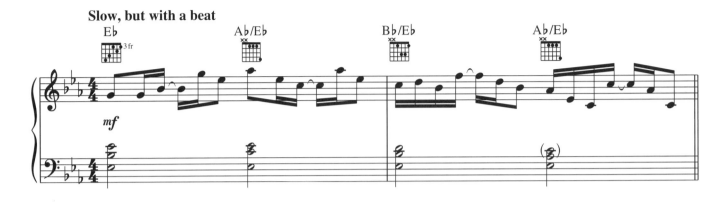

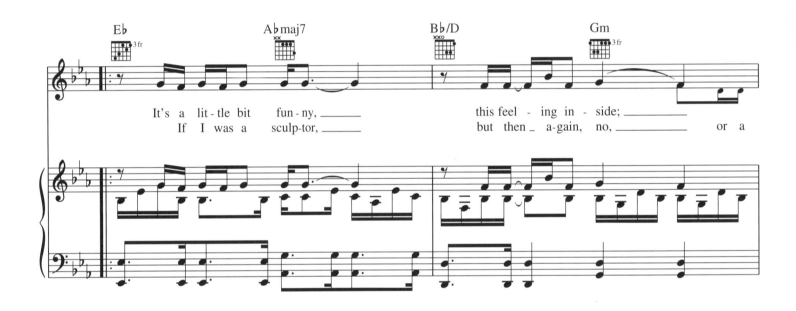

It's a lit - tle bit fun - ny, _____ this feel - ing in - side; _____
If I was a sculp - tor, _____ but then _ a-gain, no, _____ or a

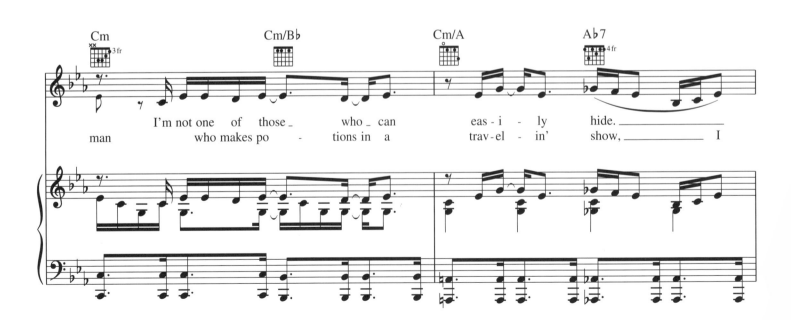

I'm not one of those _ who _ can eas - i - ly hide. _____
man who makes po - tions in a trav - el - in' show, _____ I

Copyright © 1969 UNIVERSAL/DICK JAMES MUSIC LTD.
Copyright Renewed
All Rights for the United States and Canada Controlled and Administered by UNIVERSAL - SONGS OF POLYGRAM INTERNATIONAL, INC.
All Rights Reserved   Used by Permission

that I put down in words how won-der-ful life is while

you're in the world.

you're in the world.

LEVON

Moderately slow, with a beat

Words and Music by ELTON JOHN
and BERNIE TAUPIN

Le-von wears his war wound like a crown
Le-von sells car-toon bal-loons in town

He calls his child Je - sus 'cause he likes the name
His fam - 'ly bus-'ness thrives. Je - sus blows up bal-loons all day,

and he sends him to the fin - est school in town.
Sits on the porch swing watch-ing them fly. And

Copyright © 1971 UNIVERSAL/DICK JAMES MUSIC LTD.
Copyright Renewed
All Rights for the United States and Canada Controlled and Administered by UNIVERSAL - SONGS OF POLYGRAM INTERNATIONAL, INC.
All Rights Reserved   Used by Permission

TINY DANCER

Words and Music by ELTON JOHN
and BERNIE TAUPIN

Verse

1.3. Blue - jean ba - by.___ L.___ A.___ la - dy.___
2. Je - sus freaks___ out in___ the___ street___

Seam - stress for___ the band.___
hand - ing tick - ets out___ for God.___

Copyright © 1971 DICK JAMES MUSIC LTD.
Copyright Renewed
All Rights in the United States and Canada Controlled and Administered by UNIVERSAL - SONGS OF POLYGRAM INTERNATIONAL, INC.
All Rights Reserved   Used by Permission

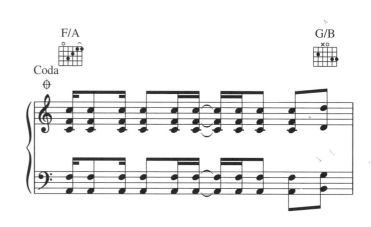

*D.S. al Coda

*On Verse repeat, take 2nd ending;
on Chorus repeat, take both endings.

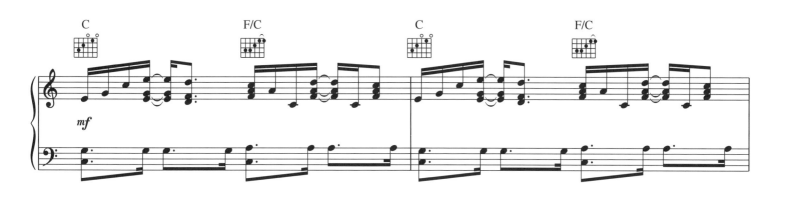

ROCKET MAN
(I Think It's Gonna Be a Long Long Time)

Moderately slow, with a beat

Words and Music by ELTON JOHN
and BERNIE TAUPIN

Copyright © 1972 UNIVERSAL/DICK JAMES MUSIC LTD.
Copyright Renewed
All Rights for the United States and Canada Controlled and Administered by UNIVERSAL - SONGS OF POLYGRAM INTERNATIONAL, INC.
All Rights Reserved   Used by Permission

HONKY CAT

Words and Music by ELTON JOHN
and BERNIE TAUPIN

Brightly, with spirit

(Xylophone)

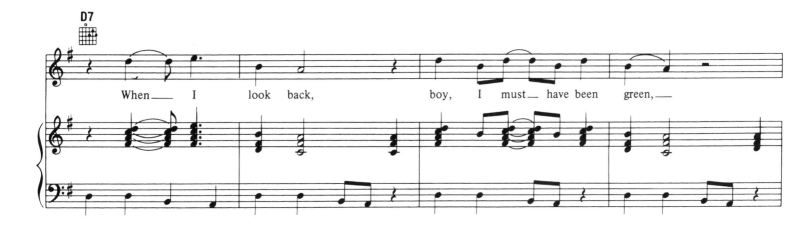

When___ I look back, boy, I must___ have been green,___

bop-pin' in the coun-try, fish-in' in___ a stream.___

Copyright © 1972 UNIVERSAL/DICK JAMES MUSIC LTD.
Copyright Renewed
All Rights for the United States and Canada Controlled and Administered by UNIVERSAL - SONGS OF POLYGRAM INTERNATIONAL, INC.
All Rights Reserved   Used by Permission

CROCODILE ROCK

Words and Music by ELTON JOHN
and BERNIE TAUPIN

Copyright © 1972 UNIVERSAL/DICK JAMES MUSIC LTD.
Copyright Renewed
All Rights for the United States and Canada Controlled and Administered by
UNIVERSAL - SONGS OF POLYGRAM INTERNATIONAL, INC.
All Rights Reserved   Used by Permission

DANIEL

Words and Music by ELTON JOHN
and BERNIE TAUPIN

Copyright © 1972 UNIVERSAL/DICK JAMES MUSIC LTD.
Copyright Renewed
All Rights for the United States and Canada Controlled and Administered by
UNIVERSAL - SONGS OF POLYGRAM INTERNATIONAL, INC.
All Rights Reserved   Used by Permission

SATURDAY NIGHT'S ALRIGHT
(For Fighting)

Words and Music by ELTON JOHN
and BERNIE TAUPIN

With a beat

Lyrics:

(2nd) It's get-ting late__ have you seen my mates__ ma I'm
Packed pret-ty tight in here to-night__

tell me when the boys get here__ It's sev-en o'-clock__ and I
look-ing for a dol-ly to__ see me right I may use a lit-tle mus-cle to

wan-na rock wan-na get__ a bel-ly ful of beer__ My
get what I need I may sink__ a lit-tle drink and shout out she's with me__ a coup-

Copyright © 1973 UNIVERSAL/DICK JAMES MUSIC LTD.
Copyright Renewed
All Rights for the United States and Canada Controlled and Administered by UNIVERSAL - SONGS OF POLYGRAM INTERNATIONAL, INC.
All Rights Reserved   Used by Permission

GOODBYE YELLOW BRICK ROAD

Words and Music by ELTON JOHN
and BERNIE TAUPIN

Moderately slow, in 2

When are you gon - na come down   When are   you going to land
What do you think you'll do then   I bet that -'ll shoot down___ your plane___

___ I should have strayed___ on the farm___   Should have list - ened___ to my___ old man
It -'ll take you a cou - ple of vod - ka and ton - ics to set you on your feet a - gain

___ You know you can't hold___ me for - ev - er___   I did - n't sign up___ with you___
May - be you'll get___ a re - place - ment there's plen - ty like me___ to be found

Copyright © 1973 UNIVERSAL/DICK JAMES MUSIC LTD.
Copyright Renewed
All Rights for the United States and Canada Controlled and Administered by UNIVERSAL - SONGS OF POLYGRAM INTERNATIONAL, INC.
All Rights Reserved   Used by Permission

CANDLE IN THE WIND

Music by ELTON JOHN
Words by BERNIE TAUPIN

Gently, reflectively

Good-bye Nor - ma Jean, _____ though I nev - er
Lone - li - ness _____ was tough, _____ the tough - est role

knew you _____ at all you had the grace to hold your - self _____ while
you ev - er played. Hol - ly - wood cre - at - ed a su - per - star _____ and

those a - round _____ you crawled. _____ They crawled out of the
pain was the price you paid. _____ E - ven when you

Copyright © 1973 UNIVERSAL/DICK JAMES MUSIC LTD.
Copyright Renewed
All Rights for the United States and Canada Controlled and Administered by
UNIVERSAL - SONGS OF POLYGRAM INTERNATIONAL, INC.
All Rights Reserved   Used by Permission

BENNIE AND THE JETS

Words and Music by ELTON JOHN
and BERNIE TAUPIN

Slowly, deliberately

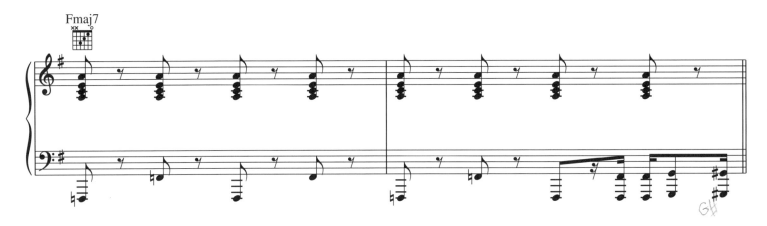

Hey, kids,__ shake__ it loose to-geth-er. The spot-light's hit-ting some-thing that's been known to change the weath-er.
Hey, kids,__ plug__ in-to the faith-less. May-be they're__ blind-ed, but Ben-nie makes them age-less.
Solo ad lib.

Copyright © 1973 UNIVERSAL/DICK JAMES MUSIC LTD.
Copyright Renewed
All Rights for the United States and Canada Controlled and Administered by
UNIVERSAL - SONGS OF POLYGRAM INTERNATIONAL, INC.
All Rights Reserved   Used by Permission

Ben-nie,   Ben-nie,   Ben-nie,   Ben-nie   and the Jets. ____

DON'T LET THE SUN GO DOWN ON ME

Words and Music by ELTON JOHN
and BERNIE TAUPIN

Copyright © 1974 by Big Pig Music Ltd.
Copyright Renewed
All Rights for the United States Administered by Intersong U.S.A., Inc.
International Copyright Secured   All Rights Reserved

THE BITCH IS BACK

Words and Music by ELTON JOHN
and BERNIE TAUPIN

With a driving beat

Copyright © 1974 by Big Pig Music Ltd.
Copyright Renewed
All Rights for the United States Administered by Intersong U.S.A., Inc.
International Copyright Secured   All Rights Reserved

PHILADELPHIA FREEDOM

Words and Music by ELTON JOHN
and BERNIE TAUPIN

Copyright © 1975 by Big Pig Music Ltd.
Copyright Renewed
All Rights for the United States Administered by Intersong U.S.A., Inc.
International Copyright Secured   All Rights Reserved

Additional Lyrics

2. If you choose to, you can live your life alone.
   Some people choose the city,
   Some others choose the good old family home.
   I like living easy without family ties,
   'Til the whippoorwill of freedom zapped me
   Right between the eyes.

Repeat Chorus

SOMEONE SAVED MY LIFE TONIGHT

Words and Music by ELTON JOHN
and BERNIE TAUPIN

Copyright © 1975 by Big Pig Music Ltd.
Copyright Renewed
All Rights for the United States Administered by Intersong U.S.A., Inc.
International Copyright Secured   All Rights Reserved

Verse 2. I never realized the passing hours
Of evening showers,
A slip noose hanging in my darkest dreams.
I'm strangled by your haunted social scene
Just a pawn out-played by a dominating queen.
It's four-o-clock in the morning
Damn it!
Listen to me good.
I'm sleeping with myself tonight
Saved in time, thank God my music's still alive.
To Chorus

ISLAND GIRL

Words and Music by ELTON JOHN
and BERNIE TAUPIN

With movement

I see your teeth flash Ja-mai-can hon-ey so sweet

down where Lex-ing-ton cross for-ty sev-enth street

Oh, she's a big girl, she's stand-ing six foot three

Copyright © 1975 by Big Pig Music Ltd.
Copyright Renewed
All Rights for the United States Administered by Intersong U.S.A., Inc.
International Copyright Secured   All Rights Reserved

SORRY SEEMS TO BE THE HARDEST WORD

Words and Music by ELTON JOHN
and BERNIE TAUPIN

Slow lament

Copyright © 1976 by Big Pig Music Ltd.
All Rights for the United States Administered by Intersong U.S.A., Inc.
International Copyright Secured   All Rights Reserved

DON'T GO BREAKING MY HEART

Words and Music by CARTE BLANCHE
and ANN ORSON

Moderately

Verse

(Boy) Don't go break-ing my heart____
And no-bod-y told____ us.

(Girl) I could-n't if I tried.____
'Cause no-bod-y showed____

____ us

(Boy) Oh, hon-ey if I____ get to rest-less
And now____ it's up____ to us____ babe

Copyright © 1976 by Big Pig Music Ltd.
All Rights for the United States Administered by Intersong U.S.A., Inc.
International Copyright Secured   All Rights Reserved

86

LITTLE JEANNIE

Words and Music by ELTON JOHN
and GARY OSBORNE

Copyright © 1980 by Big Pig Music Ltd.
All Rights for the United States Administered by Intersong U.S.A., Inc.
International Copyright Secured   All Rights Reserved

I'M STILL STANDING

Words and Music by ELTON JOHN
and BERNIE TAUPIN

You could nev-er know what it's like;__ your blood like win-ter freez-es
Did you think this fool could nev-er win?__ Well, look at me, I'm com-in'
Once I nev-er could hope to win,__ you start-in' down the road and leav-in'

just like ice,__ and there's a cold lone-ly light that shines__ from you.__ You'll wind
back a-gain. I got a taste of love in a sim-ple way, and if you
me a-gain._____ The threats you made were meant to cut me down, and if our

up like the wreck you hide__ be-hind__ that mask you use.
need to know, while I'm still stand-in' you__ just fade a-way.
love__ was just__ a cir-cus, you'd be a clown by now.

Original key: B♭ major. This edition has been transposed down one half-step to be more playable.

Copyright © 1983 by Big Pig Music Ltd.
All Rights for the United States Administered by Intersong U.S.A., Inc.
International Copyright Secured   All Rights Reserved

I GUESS THAT'S WHY THEY CALL IT THE BLUES

Words and Music by ELTON JOHN,
BERNIE TAUPIN and DAVEY JOHNSTONE

Moderately slow; with a beat

Don't wish it a-way, don't look at it like it's for-
Just stare in-to space; pic-ture my face in your
Instrumental solo

ev - er.
hands.

Be - tween you ___ and
Live for ___ each

Copyright © 1983 by Big Pig Music Ltd.
All Rights for the United States Administered by Intersong U.S.A., Inc.
International Copyright Secured   All Rights Reserved

SAD SONGS
(Say So Much)

Words and Music by ELTON JOHN
and BERNIE TAUPIN

Guess there are times____ when we__ all__ need__
If some-one else is suf - fer-in'____ e - nough,

to share_____ a lit - tle pain__
oh,_____ to write____ it down__

and iron - ing out the
when ev - 'ry sin - gle

Copyright © 1984 by Big Pig Music Ltd.
All Rights for the United States Administered by Intersong U.S.A., Inc.
International Copyright Secured   All Rights Reserved

I DON'T WANNA GO ON WITH YOU LIKE THAT

Words and Music by ELTON JOHN
and BERNIE TAUPIN

I've al - ways said that one's e - nough to love. ___ Now ___

___ I hear you're brag - gin' one is not e - nough. ___

Well, some - one tells me you're not sat - is - fied. ___ You got

Copyright © 1988 by Big Pig Music Ltd.
All Rights for the United States Administered by Intersong U.S.A., Inc.
International Copyright Secured   All Rights Reserved

NIKITA

Words and Music by ELTON JOHN
and BERNIE TAUPIN

Hey, Nik - it - a, is it cold _
Do you ev - er dream of me? _

in your lit - tle cor - ner
Do you ev - er see the let - ters

of the world?
that I write?

You could roll
When you look up through the wire,

a - round the globe, _

Copyright © 1985 by Big Pig Music Ltd.
All Rights for the United States Administered by Intersong U.S.A., Inc.
International Copyright Secured   All Rights Reserved

nev - er___ know.___

SACRIFICE

Words and Music by ELTON JOHN
and BERNIE TAUPIN

It's a hu-man _ sign _____ when things _ go wrong, _
Mu-tual mis-un-der-stand - ing af - ter the fact. _

_ when the scent of her lin - gers _____ and temp - ta - tion's strong. _
_ Sen - si - tiv-i - ty builds_ a pris - on in the fi - nal act. __

Copyright © 1989 by Big Pig Music Ltd.
All Rights for the United States Administered by Intersong U.S.A., Inc.
International Copyright Secured All Rights Reserved

THE ONE

Words and Music by ELTON JOHN
and BERNIE TAUPIN

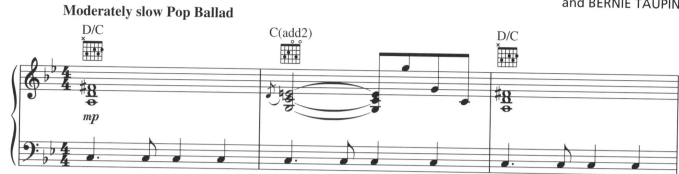

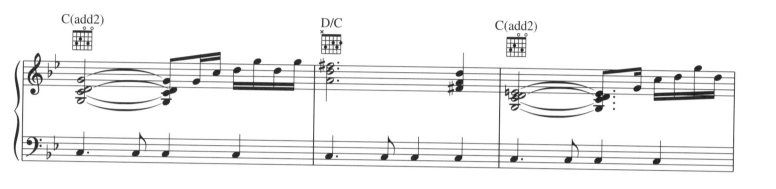

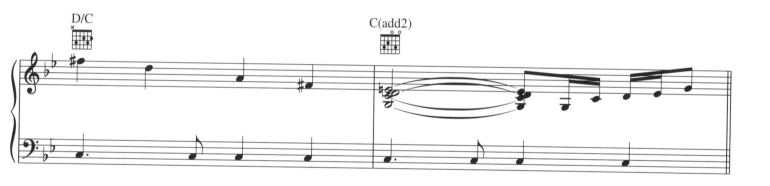

I saw you danc - in' out ___ the o - cean, ___
There are car - a - vans ___ we fol - low, ___

Copyright © 1991 by Big Pig Music Ltd.
All Rights for the United States Administered by Intersong U.S.A., Inc.
International Copyright Secured   All Rights Reserved

© 1994 Wonderland Music Company, Inc.
All Rights Reserved Used by Permission

CIRCLE OF LIFE
from Walt Disney Pictures' THE LION KING

Music by ELTON JOHN
Lyrics by TIM RICE

From the

© 1994 Wonderland Music Company, Inc.
All Rights Reserved   Used by Permission

138

BELIEVE

Words and Music by ELTON JOHN
and BERNIE TAUPIN

Copyright © 1995 by William A. Bong Limited (PRS) and Hania (ASCAP)
All Rights Administered by WB Music Corp.
International Copyright Secured   All Rights Reserved

BLESSED

Words and Music by ELTON JOHN
and BERNIE TAUPIN

Copyright © 1995 by William A. Bong Limited (PRS) and Hania (ASCAP)
All Rights Administered by WB Music Corp.
International Copyright Secured All Rights Reserved

SOMETHING ABOUT THE WAY YOU LOOK TONIGHT

Words and Music by ELTON JOHN
and BERNIE TAUPIN

Original Key: F-sharp major. This edition has been transposed down one half-step to be more playable.

Copyright © 1996 by William A. Bong Limited (PRS) and Wretched Music (ASCAP)
All Rights for William A. Bong Limited Administered by Warner-Tamerlane Publishing Corp. (BMI)
All Rights for Wretched Music Administered by WB Music Corp. (ASCAP)
International Copyright Secured   All Rights Reserved

WRITTEN IN THE STARS

from Walt Disney Theatrical Productions' AIDA

Music by ELTON JOHN
Lyrics by TIM RICE

© 1999 Wonderland Music Company, Inc., Happenstance Ltd. and Evadon Ltd.
All Rights Reserved   Used by Permission

To Coda

fail _____ to un-der-stand   how a per-fect love __ can be con-found - ed
wish _____ I nev-er learned   what it is to be __ in love   and have that

out of hand. _____ (Both:) Is it   writ-ten in the stars? ____   Are we

pay - ing for some crime? _   Is that all   that we are good for, __   just a

stretch of mor-tal time? _____   Is this God's ex-per-i-ment ____   in

I WANT LOVE

Words and Music by ELTON JOHN
and BERNIE TAUPIN

Copyright © 2001 by Happenstance Limited and Wretched Music
All Rights in the U.S. Administered by WB Music Corp.
All Rights outside the U.S. Administered by Muziekuitgeverij Artemis B.V.
International Copyright Secured   All Rights Reserved

THIS TRAIN DON'T STOP THERE ANYMORE

Words and Music by ELTON JOHN
and BERNIE TAUPIN

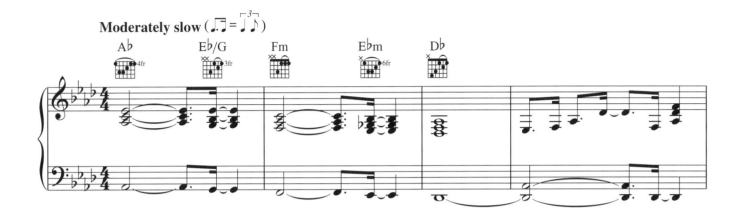

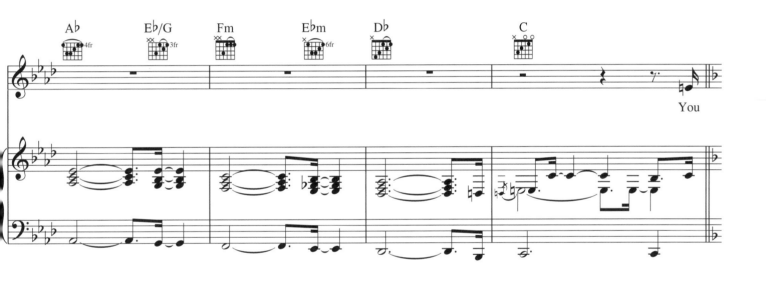

You

may not ___ be-lieve it, but I don't be-lieve in mir-ac-les ___ a-ny-more.

don't need ___ to hear it, but I'm dried up and sick to death of love.

Copyright © 2001 by Happenstance Limited and Wretched Music
All Rights for Happenstance Limited in the U.S. Administered by Warner-Tamerlane Publishing Corp.
All Rights for Wretched Music in the U.S. Administered by WB Music Corp.
International Copyright Secured   All Rights Reserved